How to use this book

Follow the advice, in italics, given for you on each page.
Support the children as they read the text that is shaded in cream.
Praise *the children at every step!*

Detailed guidance is provided in the Read Write Inc. Phonics Handbook

8 reading activities

Children:
- *Practise reading the speed sounds.*
- *Read the green and red words for the story.*
- *Listen as you read the introduction.*
- *Discuss the vocabulary check with you.*
- *Read the story.*
- *Re-read the story and discuss the 'questions to talk about'.*
- *Re-read the story with fluency and expression.*
- *Practise reading the speed words.*

Speed sounds

Consonants *Say the pure sounds (do not add 'uh').*

f ff	l ll	m mm	n (nn) kn	r rr	s ss (se)	v ve	z zz s	sh	th	ng nk

b bb	c k ck	d dd	g gg	h	j	p pp	qu	t tt	w wh	x	y	ch tch

Vowels *Say the sounds in and out of order.* *emphasise both 'oi' and 'oy'*

at	hen head	in	on	up	day	see happy	high	blow

zoo	look	car	for door snore	fair	whirl	shout	boy spoil

*Each box contains one sound but sometimes more than one grapheme. Focus graphemes are **circled**.*

Read in Fred Talk (pure sounds).

slow   far   lunch

boy   Floyd   Roy   Toya   Troy   point   join

Read in syllables.

tor`toise   sand`pit   Sun`day

Read the root word first and then with the ending.

point → pointed   look → looked

Red words

he   be   said   no   so   go   to   all   call   the

Vocabulary check

Discuss the meaning (as used in the story) after the children have read each word.

definition:

hunt	*search*
greenhouse	*a warm glass house where plants are grown*
tortoise	*a slow moving creature with a large protective shell*

Punctuation to note in this story:

Troy Grandad Mum **Floyd Roy Toya**	*Capital letters for names*
He The On We Let's	*Capital letters that start sentences*
.	*Full stop at the end of each sentence*

Hunt the tortoise

Introduction

Who has got a pet?
What do you think about having a tortoise as a pet?

Troy owns a tortoise (exaggerate 'oi' in tortoise) called Floyd. Unfortunately, one day when his family is having a picnic, Floyd disappears.

Will Troy ever see Floyd again?

Story written by Gill Munton
Illustrated by Tim Archbold

Troy is a lucky boy.

He has got a tortoise!

The tortoise is called Floyd.

On Sunday, Floyd got lost.

"He cannot be far away," said Mum.

"He is too slow to go far."

"Let's go on a tortoise hunt,"

said Grandpa Roy.

"We can all join in."

So Mum,   and Grandpa Roy,   and Toya,

and Troy

all went on a tortoise hunt.

Mum looked in

the greenhouse.

No tortoise.

Grandpa Roy looked

in the weeds.

No tortoise.

Toya looked in the sandpit.

No tortoise.

Then Troy pointed

to Mum's lunch.

Questions to talk about

FIND IT

✓ *Turn to the page*

✓ *Read the question*

✓ *Find the answer*

PROVE IT

✓ *Turn to the page*

✓ *Read the question*

✓ *Find your evidence*

✓ *Explain why*

Page 8:	FIND IT	*Why is Troy a lucky boy?*
Page 9:	FIND IT	*Why did Mum say that Floyd could not be far away?*
Page 10:	FIND IT	*What did Grandpa Roy suggest they do?*
Page 11:	FIND IT	*Who went on the tortoise hunt?*
Page 12:	FIND IT	*Where did Mum and Grandpa Roy look?*
Page 13:	FIND IT	*Why did Troy point to Mum's lunch?*
Page 13:	FIND IT	*What is Floyd thinking?*